Quick Coach Guide
to
Avoiding Plagiarism

Rosemarie Menager, Ed.D.
Foothill College

Lyn Paulos
Santa Barbara City College

WADSWORTH
CENGAGE Learning™

Australia • Brazil • Japan • Korea • Mexico • Singapore • Spain • United Kingdom • United States

WADSWORTH
CENGAGE Learning™

Quick Coach Guide to Avoiding Plagiarism
Rosemarie Menager
Lyn Paulos

Senior Publisher: Lyn Uhl

Executive Editor: Monica Eckman

Acquisitions Editor: Margaret Leslie

Assistant Editor: Amy Haines

Editorial Assistant: Elizabeth Ramsey

Media Editor: Cara Douglass-Graff/Janine Tangney

Marketing Manager: Jennifer Zourdos

Marketing Coordinator: Ryan Ahern

Marketing Communications Manager: Stacey Purviance

Content Project Manager: Corinna Dibble

Senior Art Director: Jill Ort

Senior Print Buyer: Betsy Donaghey

Permissions Editor: Jennifer Meyer Dare

Production Service: Pre-Press PMG

Compositor: Pre-Press PMG

For product information and technology assistance, contact us at **Cengage Learning Customer & Sales Support, 1-800-354-9706**

For permission to use material from this text or product, submit all requests online at **www.cengage.com/permissions.** Further permissions questions can be emailed to **permissionrequest@cengage.com.**

Library of Congress Control Number: 2010923870

ISBN-13: 978-1-111-34246-3

ISBN-10: 1-111-34246-6

Wadsworth
20 Channel Center Street
Boston, MA 02210
USA

Cengage Learning is a leading provider of customized learning solutions with office locations around the globe, including Singapore, the United Kingdom, Australia, Mexico, Brazil, and Japan. Locate your local office at **international.cengage.com/region**

Cengage Learning products are represented in Canada by Nelson Education, Ltd.

For your course and learning solutions, visit **www.cengage.com.**

Purchase any of our products at your local college store or at our preferred online store **www.CengageBrain.com.**

Printed in the United States of America
5 6 7 14

Contents
The Quick Coach Guide to Avoiding Plagiarism

Preface

"It is better to fail in originality than
to succeed in imitation."

Herman Melville (1819–1891)

This guide is the culmination of years of working with students and their writing assignments in classrooms, learning labs, and online classes. When students were caught using the writing and research of others—plagiarizing—we found most cases to involve students with weak writing, poor English skills, or students who did not understand how to use citations. Rather than see students make uninformed mistakes that were setbacks to their education and future, we looked for ways to help them successfully author their own work and avoid plagiarizing.

As educators, we emphasized the educational aspects instead of academic integrity. We did not want to be punitive to our students. Our goal was to prevent them from making citation errors in the first place and getting punished for what was really not intentional. By making sure students had the knowledge to create honest work, we could improve their skills and motivation, reducing the incidents of plagiarism in our classes. This also made it much easier to separate the honest students from those who were not. Once we employed this model, the students we caught plagiarizing knew what they were doing. It became obvious that an educational approach weeded out the accidental cheaters from the intentional cheaters, making honor code enforcement easier.

Student response to the educational model of academic integrity has been excellent and this guide is the result. We hope it helps students learn the importance of doing honest work and gives them the necessary tools to write essays, reports, term papers, and the like with pride and confidence.

ABOUT THE AUTHORS

Rosemarie Menager, Ed.D. is a psychology professor at Foothill College. A graduate of USC's Rossiter School of Education Human Performance Technology cohort, she did her dissertation on student success in online learning. After discovering that many of her students were inadvertently plagiarizing because they lacked a clear understanding of how to correctly cite their work, Dr. Menager created "Educate First and Enforce Next," an educational approach to preventing plagiarism that informs the content of this *Quick Coach Guide.* Dr. Menager has also served as a consultant for the "Stressed-Out Student (SOS)" conference at Stanford University and is currently working on a plagiarism intervention for students in grades K-12. In her spare time, Dr. Menager is a mom, impressionist oil painter, and member of a sheriff's mounted search and rescue group.

Lyn Paulos is an assistive technology lab technician at Santa Barbara City College. She is currently completing her B.S. in psychology and will be pursuing an M.S. through the University of Phoenix. Ms. Paulos currently manages a state-of-the art adaptive technology learning lab at Santa Barbara City College. A frequent presenter at technology conferences and passionate advocate for student academic integrity, she has also authored an online tutorial on plagiarism prevention and education entitled "Authoring Your Own Work." In her extracurricular life, Ms. Paulos is a celebrated lampwork glass artist whose creations are collected internationally.

1

Introduction

IN THIS GUIDE

This guide is designed to help students avoid the pitfalls of plagiarism. The chapters cover the correct way to credit sources, quote, cite, paraphrase, summarize, create a list of references, and more. *Knowledge Checks* are provided at the end of each section for your review.

WHY THIS GUIDE IS IMPORTANT

What do you want from college? There are many answers to this question, and certainly one of them is to succeed in your coursework. Probably the last thing you would want is to fail a class for cheating or plagiarizing by mistake. If you are unfamiliar with the practices and rules of incorporating work from other sources, then you will find this short guide useful. We've tried to make the information and skills you need clear and simple.

You can use the *Knowledge Checks* at the end of the main chapters and the final quiz to practice all the skills necessary to correctly use and cite your research material. Citing your sources—what to cite, when, how—can be confusing. Most colleges have very specific requirements about giving references, depending on the subject or instructor. Correct citation is more involved than just inserting footnotes or listing references at the end of a paper. Including punctuation with quotes, using extracts, and a number of other considerations are necessary to distinguish your sources from your writing. This guide provides information and samples of the kinds of citations that are necessary to correctly reference different types of academic work.

DEFINING PLAGIARISM

Plagiarism is using someone else's work and passing it off as one's own. The term comes from the Latin word *plagiarius*, which means *kidnapper*. It also has another root word in Greek, *plagios*, which means *crooked* or *treacherous*. (*Reader's Digest Great Encyclopedic Dictionary* 1031).

This means that if a student uses another writer's work without giving credit, it may be considered deceptive, even if it is an honest mistake. Knowing the definition of plagiarism and when to cite sources is the best way to avoid problems.

Preventing plagiarism is also a critical part of the academic integrity that is expected, or even required, by educational institutions. Many schools and colleges have well-defined codes of honor or conduct that prohibit dishonesty, including cheating and plagiarizing. You should be aware of the rules and consequences for dishonesty in your academic setting.

The right to protect and profit from one's originality was recognized and codified by the founders of this country. Regulations about ownership and the right to profit from an individual's creations, including written work, is in Article 1, Section 8 of the U.S. Constitution, Title 17 of the U.S. Code, and parts of other copyright laws. Violators of copyright laws have faced severe consequences, including legal prosecution, loss of jobs, and damage to their reputations. Newspaper editors, college presidents, professors, and many other successful professionals have been discredited and subject to severe penalties for plagiarism. Countries that want to profit from originality must also respect it and enforce owners' rights. Some countries consider it a moral imperative as well as a commercial right (Chavez 127). There are many practical reasons for academic integrity, as well. Your safety, and confidence in doctors, mechanics, and other service providers might be in serious question if you did not assume they had integrity and honesty.

UNDERSTANDING WHEN TO GIVE CREDIT

Because information, pictures, and music are now easy to copy from the Internet, it's more tempting than ever to find and freely use those materials. How can you tell when it is appropriate to use something without a citation and when it isn't?

Generally, any time you use someone else's work as a source of ideas or inspiration, credit is required. There are a few exceptions, such as when the information is common knowledge. An example of common knowledge is the fact that Christopher Columbus crossed the Atlantic Ocean in 1492. To be safe, if you consult a source and that source's ideas become part of your work, then you need to cite that source. If you use a direct quotation, then you need to reproduce it accurately and cite it correctly. These practices prevent inadvertent plagiarizing, and this guide provides the basics to get you started.

Tip
When you consult a source, cite it correctly.

There are also limitations on how much of someone else's work can be used as part of an assignment. Exclusively, excessively, or inappropriately using another author's work by copying, paraphrasing, summarizing, or directly quoting is plagiarizing. It is important to use your own words and ideas in a paper. One suggested rule of thumb for the acceptable amount of outside source content to use in an assignment is no more than 10 percent provided it is properly cited (Zaharoff). Make sure to check your instructor's preferences.

Many students worry that their own words do not sound as professional as those used by the original author. The point of using a source in the first place is to give you an opportunity to bring in outside authorities to support your *own* ideas, as expressed in your *own* words. Instructors do not give assignments so that students can give them back in someone else's words. Instructors want to read *your words*. If instructors wanted to read only the professional author's words and ideas, they could go directly to the original source and skip yours. It's important for you to work with ideas and to express them in writing so that you can develop your own writing style, perspective, voice, and analytical skills. This is a big investment of time and effort. Often when students risk plagiarizing, they haven't allowed themselves sufficient time to complete an assignment. This miscalculation can lead to trouble.

> **Tip**
> Know the rules about plagiarism; ignorance is no excuse.

KNOWING THE RULES

Because academic integrity and the validity of a college degree are vitally important to institutions of higher learning, schools create codes and policies governing instances of dishonesty. These policies come under various headings: Academic Integrity, Academic Honesty, Honor Code, Cheating, Student Conduct Code, or Plagiarism. They list rules, definitions, and specific behaviors that are considered cheating. These codes also describe consequences and the various procedures that occur when a student is caught cheating. **It is your responsibility to know the rules of your institution and to follow them.** Rules are usually published in school catalogs and are considered a part of the enrollment agreement for the college. If you have any questions about academic policies, check with your instructor or the dean's office to get the facts.

When instructors suspect plagiarism, they are obligated to follow steps prescribed by the institution to address the problem. These steps include contacting the student and forwarding a report to the dean or a disciplinary committee, and a possible hearing before either or both.

Consequences to the student can include failing the assignment or even the entire course. Some institutions assign community service or some other restitution to the campus community as part of the punishment. Some students have been unhappily surprised to learn that the consequences for a first-time offense of plagiarism can be as severe as expulsion. Being caught as a plagiarizer is humiliating and can also be costly. It can directly affect a student's progress toward a degree. And it is entirely avoidable.

Don't gamble with your academic future. Taking this risk with the expectation that you won't get caught can result in consequences much worse than a warning or a simple failing grade on an assignment. This kind of high-stakes gambling can make you a loser. Keep the odds in your favor. If you aren't prepared, it's better to get a poor grade on one assignment than to fail in a class (or worse) because you panicked and plagiarized.

Knowledge Check

True or False?

1. Most students who plagiarize do so inadvertently. T/F

2. Students cannot be accused of plagiarizing if they don't know the citation style expected by the instructor. T/F

3. Using sources for educational purposes means that those sources are exempt from citation rules. T/F

Check your answers on page 54.

2
Avoiding Plagiarism

This chapter lists and describes twelve guidelines to help you avoid plagiarizing, good practices when writing a paper:

1. Do your own work and use your own words.
2. Allow yourself enough time to research the assignment.
3. Keep careful track of your sources.
4. Take careful notes.
5. Make it clear who is speaking.
6. Credit the source.
7. Cite sources correctly.
8. Quote accurately and sparingly.
9. Paraphrase and cite.
10. Do not patchwrite.
11. Summarize.
12. Avoid using other students' papers and paper mills.

DOING YOUR OWN WORK, USING YOUR OWN WORDS

College gives you the opportunity to be exposed to new ideas, to formulate ideas of your own, and to develop the skills necessary to communicate your ideas. Strengthening your writing skills requires hard work and practice, but you learn thinking and communicating skills that will benefit both your studies in college and your career.

Expressing a thought in your own words may seem overwhelming. The difficulty may stem from not understanding the language, not understanding the research material, or lacking confidence in expressing ideas and concepts. Don't be discouraged by the thought that your paper may not sound as professional as you would like. By creating and practicing your own personal style, you improve your ability to state ideas clearly and support your arguments, as well as increase your vocabulary.

These skills are not built by using another researcher's or student's words or by paying a service to write a paper for your class. Attempting to cheat on your paper cheats you the most because you are depriving yourself of the thinking, learning, and writing practice that benefits every aspect of your education and beyond.

Cheating also creates the risk of humiliation and punishment. Most professors are so familiar with the work in their field that they can spot a fake quickly. New plagiarism detection methods are also making it easier for professors to catch cheaters electronically. Finally, as discussed in Chapter 1, all institutions punish students who plagiarize. Doing honest work is the way to avoid the negative consequences of cheating.

ALLOWING ENOUGH TIME

Often, students caught plagiarizing claim that they didn't have time to do the work. This excuse rarely works. Allow sufficient time to do all the steps necessary in an assignment. The best way is to plan for each part: selecting the topic, doing the research, then writing and refining your ideas. Minimizing the time it will take to do the work, or procrastinating because you feel that you do better work when you are anxious, more often than not leads to trouble.

The most productive strategy is to begin the assignment as soon as it is given and try to complete it early. This allows you to adjust the schedule if you encounter any research difficulties, provides time for questions or clarification, and offsets other events that can interfere or cut into study time. If you are unsure about how to plot out your time for each step, then ask your instructor to help you plan your schedule.

KEEPING TRACK OF SOURCES

As you look through books, articles, online sources, and other materials, you will be able to identify which content is relevant to your paper. The sources from which you decide to take notes are the ones for which you will need to keep careful records.

Create a master list of all your sources that contains detailed bibliographic information for each item. (You need to record the author, the title of the source, its publisher, the date, and page number. Chapter 6 has more detailed information on what to cite and how to format it.) As you conduct your research, you will likely add or delete sources from this list, but keeping it current and complete will make your work much easier when it comes time to format your list of Works Cited or References. This list of references enables your readers to locate the exact content you discuss in your paper—as well as assists you in finding it again.

TAKING NOTES

Some students find they take better and more easily referenced notes if they make photocopies of relevant pages from their sources. If you decide to use this method for print sources such as articles and books, photocopy the copyright page and make a copy of the relevant table of contents pages for each source. Make sure the page numbers or other identifiers are visible on each page. For electronic sources, such as websites, databases,

CDs, or even blogs, print out both the home or copyright page and the relevant content pages, making sure that identifiers such as page numbers—and (for online sources) the URL and access date—are visible.

If you take notes instead on note cards or in computer files, then make sure to keep a detailed record of where each note came from and take down the information carefully and accurately.

Next, scrutinize your resources, thinking about the ideas expressed, noting and recording the relevant points, and adding to the notes your reactions, questions, and thoughts. If you find a particular phrase that you want to quote, then highlight it to separate it from the regular notes.

CLARIFYING WHO IS SPEAKING

As you write the first draft of your paper, make sure you express your thoughts and ideas in your own voice. Use the thoughts or words of others only to support your thoughts, not to make your point for you. Your writing should make clear at all times who is speaking.

Decide from your notes whether you need to quote, summarize, or paraphrase the source. (Chapters 3, 4, and 5 discuss each method.) Then make sure to introduce the guest voice (the source) and explain why the source's information is relevant to your topic.

CREDITING THE SOURCE

When you draft your paper, if you are stating another person's thought, make the source or origin of that thought clear. Identify the source of any and all borrowed content in your paper. Your readers need to know where to find the original source if they want to explore the idea further.

The academic departments of virtually every college and university recommend that their students use a particular style guide. The guides issued by the Modern Language Association (MLA) and the American Psychological Association (APA), as well as the University of Chicago's *Manual of Style* (CMS), are the most common. Each features a method to identify your source by inserting a brief parenthetical citation where the source's content appears and then creating a list with the complete source information placed at the end of the paper. Follow whichever style your instructor specifies.

CITING SOURCES CORRECTLY

A citation—a statement of the source of an idea, a conclusion, or a specific collection of information—of another person's work is the highest form of respect that a serious writer can make. It is also the single best way to avoid accusations of plagiarism and cheating. Properly citing sources involves acknowledging them both in the body of your work (when and where your writing borrows from a given source) and in a list of all the sources at the end of your paper.

Check with your instructor or writing center for the proper format style of your writing project. Citation styles differ by subject or discipline—and many overlap in the areas of study and writing for which they were originally intended. For English and the other humanities, the MLA style is typically used. Psychology, Sociology, Business, Economics, and similar disciplines typically follow APA. More specialized style guides exist for other disciplines, including the Council of Science Editors (CSE) style, which is used in scientific writing.

Chapters 3 through 5 discuss how to use parenthetical citations and quotations, paraphrases, and summaries (respectively). Chapter 6 surveys the various methods of

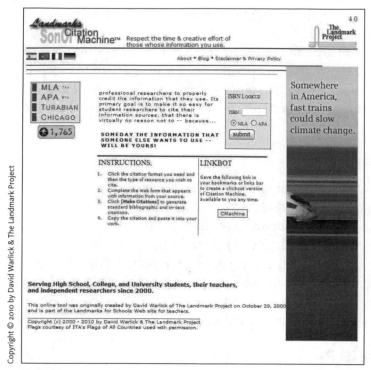

This is the main page for a free online citation generator that helps create citations in different styles.

compiling references as well as presenting basic examples. For more detailed information, you can purchase the style guides for MLA, APA, and CMS styles, available at most bookstores. Online citation generators can also help you with listing references in the correct format.

QUOTING

Quotations should be used only to emphasize your point, which you have already stated in your own words. A good quotation from an original source can underscore a theme and introduce thoughts or direction, but quotations should be relevant, necessary, accurate, and limited.

Using too many direct quotations (more than ten percent) is a sign both that you have not developed your own idea enough and that you are relying on others to make your point for you. Over-quoting is also an opportunity for plagiarism to creep in. If you are using several sources, then limit how much those sources contribute, and give a correct citation and credit every time you use them.

PARAPHRASING

The practice of taking another writer's sentence and then looking up words and replacing them with synonyms is a common way for students to think they are paraphrasing from a source (see Chapter 4). Merely changing some of another writer's words, or reversing the order of the clauses in the sentences, is still copying. This is another way you can inadvertently plagiarize. Use paraphrase to state in your own words what another writer believes or argues.

AVOIDING PATCHWRITING

Patchwriting consists of mixing several references together and arranging paraphrases and quotations to constitute much of a paper. In essence, the student has assembled others' works—with a bit of embroidery here and there—but with very little original thought or expression. Work that has been simply patched together is very likely to contain plagiarism.

To avoid patchwriting, develop a position and bring in sources only as needed to support your viewpoint or argument. Read the material several times to make sure you understand what the source is saying. Then put it aside and think about it. Analyze the readings and what they mean, and then try to organize the main points. Create an outline of what you want to say and go back and pull in the supporting information from the sources. Good writers think of the reader as listening to what is being said; this process will help you create and organize your own original work and find your own voice in your writing.

SUMMARIZING

Most word processors have an automatic summarize function that can take 50 pages and turn them into ten. The problem with this feature is that it condenses material by selecting key sentences. Therefore, a summarized version is still in the exact words of the original source, only shorter, and does not necessarily make the same point as the original. The auto-summary feature is intended for writers to summarize their own work, not the work of others. If a paper uses any portion of an auto-summary generated from another writer's work, then it is plagiarism.

If you wish to summarize another writer's work, then describe briefly in your own words the writer's idea, identifying who that writer is and providing a citation of the work, and state how it relates to your own ideas (see Chapter 5).

AVOIDING USING OTHER STUDENTS' PAPERS AND PAPER MILLS

Don't cross the line from looking at someone else's paper to presenting it as original work. A paper written by another student can be an example of how to do the assignment. Reworking or rewriting that person's paper for submission is plagiarism.

Similarly, buying papers from paper mills, or paying for someone else to write a paper, is obviously dishonest and is a clear example of plagiarizing. Databases of written papers are often kept by colleges and by plagiarism detection services, so instructors who question the authenticity of a student's paper can easily verify its source.

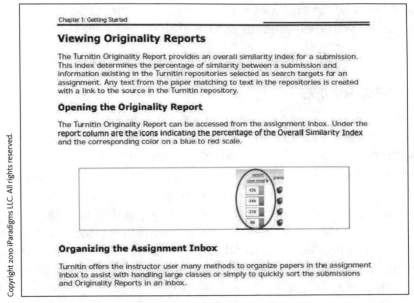

Chapter 1: Getting Started

Viewing Originality Reports

The Turnitin Originality Report provides an overall similarity index for a submission. This index determines the percentage of similarity between a submission and information existing in the Turnitin repositories selected as search targets for an assignment. Any text from the paper matching to text in the repositories is created with a link to the source in the Turnitin repository.

Opening the Originality Report

The Turnitin Originality Report can be accessed from the assignment inbox. Under the report column are the icons indicating the percentage of the Overall Similarity Index and the corresponding color on a blue to red scale.

Organizing the Assignment Inbox

Turnitin offers the instructor user many methods to organize papers in the assignment inbox to assist with handling large classes or simply to quickly sort the submissions and Originality Reports in an inbox.

Turnitin's® "Originality Reports" help faculty detect plagiarism in student papers.

Knowledge Check

True or False?

1.   One way to avoid plagiarizing is to give yourself enough time to do a good job on the assignment. T/F

2.   As long as you put everything in quotation marks, you are not plagiarizing. T/F

3.   Getting a paper from a friend or the Internet is a good way to get a head start on your assignment. T/F

Check your answers on page 54.

3

Quotations and
Parenthetical Citations

UNDERSTANDING CITATIONS

This chapter shows you how to use the work of others and
correctly credit it in the body of your own. Citation is an
accolade to the original writer and a way to acknowledge his or
her influence on your research or thinking. It is also the single
best way to avoid accusations of plagiarism and cheating.
"Plagiarizing doesn't just mean borrowing someone else's words.
It also means borrowing someone else's ideas" (Lipson 46). The
general policy in acknowledging sources is to cite a source if
it had an influence on your work. This allows people who read
your work to follow a path back to original ideas and sources.
Citation of sources can be a very confusing process.

There are different styles of citations for different areas of
academics. You have already learned that **MLA** style is
commonly used for English, literature, and other humanities
classes. **APA** style is used for psychological research, sociology,
and even environmental science. There are other styles specialized
for math, physics, chemistry, and other disciplines. The styles
have many things in common. In this guide, we present the basics
of the MLA and APA styles, which both employ the **author-date**
convention. While this guide will not cover all the nuances of
each style—you should consult their respective guides in print and
online—it will give you an introduction.

There are several basic rules to citations. These rules include
such things as alphabetizing author lists including their names
and publications, and also specify what should be cited and how.

Knowing these rules and the basics of different citation forms will help you to properly cite your sources and give credit to the authors that have helped you and influenced your work.

While these styles have things in common, fundamental differences exist in presentation and format. For example, one style will use italics for the title of a book or journal in your paper, while another has you underline these same elements. If you have the option of either, you must choose one and be consistent. As we examine the different styles, take note that while the basic information presented in different styles can be the same, the order of presentation can be quite different.

Tip

Always check with your instructor for the style format he or she prefers.

Citation styles contain basically the same information, just in different formats. The basic information that is included in all citations styles follows:

- Author's name
- Article title
- Book title
- Publisher information
- Year of publication
- Place of publication
- Page numbers when applicable

Listings of References or Works Cited for all styles are placed at the end of the paper. They are often separated from the body of the paper on a separate page or pages—and each listing is typically set with a hanging indent so that the author names can easily be seen. (Examples of how to create reference lists are given in Chapter 6.)

USING PARENTHETICAL CITATIONS

We have already mentioned that citations are presented at the end of your work, but you need to indicate within the written text or body of the work what references are being used at any given instance. A bibliography, in which you only list the works you researched to compose your paper, is typically not enough for higher-level coursework. Correctly noting or referencing begins in the body of the text and points to the full citation at the end of the work. If you use an idea, paraphrase, or direct or indirect quote, you need to insert a **parenthetical citation**. Parenthetical citations can be considered the roadmap to your Works Cited or References list. There are several ways in which to acknowledge your sources correctly. Only work that is cited in the body of the paper is included in the list at the end. Some examples of how to use parenthetical citations with quotations follow. (There are additional examples of parenthetical citations for paraphrasing and summarizing in Chapters 4 and 5, respectively.)

Quotations with parenthetical citations

Using quotations is an effective way to support your arguments and add credibility to your research paper. Quotations are most useful when they highlight or help to refine a point you are making. However, you should quote selectively and sparingly. Inserting too many quotations in your paper distracts your readers from the argument you are trying to construct and makes your paper sound as if others are speaking for you.

You can **use a direct quotation** (a word-for-word repetition from another source) or an **indirect quotation** (a restating in your own words of the ideas of another person, which is also called paraphrasing). Each time you insert a direct or indirect quotation into your paper, you must add a citation to the source following the quotation. The necessary citation is called a parenthetical citation because of the use of parenthesis and a brief reference to the source within the referenced, quoted, or paraphrased text. A parenthetical citation, used after a quotation, may look like the following.

The following is a parenthetical citation that uses APA style:

(Houston, 2008, p. 323)

This is an MLA version of a parenthetical citation:

(Houston 323)

Both in-text citations are for direct quotation and follow an abbreviated, parenthetical format that points the reader to the full citation in a Works Cited or References list at the end of the paper (see Chapter 6).

Quotations can be used in various ways within a research paper. This chapter will cover some of those uses and the proper citation styles needed for each. Some examples of how to use parenthetical citations with quotations are included.

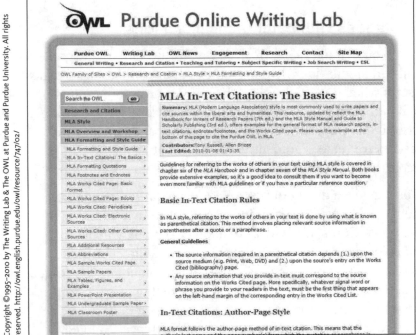

Many college websites, such as the OWL at Purdue University, provide information on preparing citations.

Follow these basic rules for using quotations:

- Use quotations sparingly.

- Make sure the quotation exactly fits the idea of your paragraph.

- Make sure direct quotations stay identical to the original passage. Do not change the wording, the spelling, or the punctuation of the original passage.

- Cite the source! Include a parenthetical citation for all quotations.

- If a direct quotation is longer than four lines, use a block quotation.

USING DIRECT QUOTATIONS

A direct quotation is an exact copy of the original author's work. Make your point first, and then enclose the quote in quotation marks (or if it is long, set it apart as a block quotation) and provide a parenthetical citation directly after.

The MLA style of citing a quotation includes the author's last name followed by the page number directly after the quotation. Note that no comma separates the name from the page number.

> Personal growth is a painful process, and part of that process is taking personal responsibility for your actions. This includes remembering that "you can't talk your way out of problems you behaved yourself into" (Covey 186).

The APA style of citing the same quotation includes the publication year as well as the author's last name and page number. Note that no comma separates the name from the date, but that a comma does follow the date and that the abbreviation "p." precedes the page number.

> Personal growth is a painful process, and part of that process is taking personal responsibility for your actions.

This includes remembering that "you can't talk your way out of problems you behaved yourself into" (Covey 1989, p. 186).

Notice that in both cases the citation is included in the sentence, with the period after the citation.

Alternatively, you can introduce the name of the author in the text and then cite the page number for reference.

Noted author Stephen Covey suggests that to be effective, one must "begin with the end in mind" (97).

Note that the APA style includes the year of publication directly after the author's name and the page number at the end for easy reference.

Weeks (1994) believes that "we need to celebrate diversity, not fear it or perceive it as a threat" (33).

USING INDIRECT QUOTATIONS

When using research sources, it is common to find that the original author has quoted a **secondary source**, another author, in his or her work. The following example shows such a quotation and the proper citation for it.

In MLA style, the addition of "qtd. in" (abbreviated for "quoted in") shows that a quote (in this case, by Jung) was found in a secondary resource (here, Byrne).

Psychology has had its masters of theory and quite a bit of humor as well. C. G. Jung, a noted psychologist, once claimed, "Show me a sane man and I will cure him for you" (Jung, qtd. in Byrne 453).

In APA style, notice the change in wording as well as the addition of the date the source was published.

Psychology has had its masters of theory and quite a bit of humor as well. C. G. Jung, a noted psychologist, once claimed, "Show me a sane man and I will cure him for you" (as cited in Byrne, 1996).

USING ELLIPSES AND BRACKETS

An **ellipsis** (shown by three evenly spaced periods: [. . .]) is a break or omission of words within a direct quote. Using only part of a quotation is common practice, especially if the entire quotation is too long or cumbersome. But make sure to use ellipses cautiously so you don't present the author's words out of intended context.

> We can now plainly and painfully see that "components of human interaction . . . often lead to conflict" (Weeks 33).

Sometimes a quote is worded in a way that could read awkwardly or make an incomplete sentence when inserted in a paper. If you need to add a word or phrase within a quotation to make your sentence grammatically correct or clearer, then put brackets around your insertion.

> There are many examples of how "components of human interaction . . . [can] often lead to conflict" (Weeks 33).

In this instance the word "can" was added to clarify the thought for the reader.

USING BLOCK QUOTATIONS

A quotation from poetry, plays, or any text longer than four lines should be set apart in block quotation format. A block quotation is indented about one inch (ten spaces) from the left margin and double-spaced. A block quotation needs no quotation marks and is introduced by a complete sentence. Often a colon, rather than a period, follows the introductory words.

Tip

Block quotations do not require quotation marks.

The block quotation is introduced by a sentence that contains the author's name and ends with a colon, and uses an ellipsis to show that it is not complete. Note that the page is included in parentheses after the period for easy reference.

> As Schein and Bernstein explain, discovering you could be a twin is a shocking yet fascinating experience:
>
> > Imagine that a slightly different version of you walks into a room, looks you in the eye, and says hello in your voice. You discover that she has the same birthday, the same allergies, the same tics, and the same way of laughing. . . . This identical individual has the exact same DNA as you and is essentially your clone. (vii)

Knowledge Check

True or False?

1. Quotations must be used in original form. T/F

2. Quotation marks are required for all direct quotations. T/F

3. Brackets indicate that a word has been added that is not in the original text. T/F

Check your answers on page 54.

4
Paraphrasing

DEFINING A PARAPHRASE

A **paraphrase** is a restatement of an author's writing that uses your own words and accurately conveys the original information. You paraphrase another author's words when you want to explain the content of the quote or to maintain your own voice and rhythm in your paper. You might also paraphrase after you have introduced a source earlier in your paper and wish to continue to discuss that source's ideas without needing to quote the source verbatim.

The length of a paraphrase should be about equal to the length of the original work. (This is not to be confused with a summary—explained in Chapter 5—which describes in a few words the ideas or points made in another author's long passage or large work.) Also, a paraphrase, because it's an indirect quotation, requires a parenthetical citation, as seen in the examples that follow.

Tip

Do

1. Use your own words.

2. Present the author's ideas without changing, adding to, or deleting from the original meaning.

3. Make the paraphrase about equal in length to the original.

4. Give credit to the source.

(continued)

> *Don't*
> 1. Keep the author's sentences and just replace the words with synonyms.
> 2. Flip-flop clauses and leave the words the same.
> 3. Lose track of original sources.

GIVING CREDIT TO THE SOURCE

Restating an author's ideas accurately in your own words and writing style can be difficult. And it can be confusing to know when—and how—to add a citation. The thing to remember is this: If a sentence or idea came from an outside source, then it should be acknowledged with a parenthetical citation.

You might be tempted to shift some words around from the original, but doing so would be plagiarizing because those words and the idea still belong to the author. Remember that improving your writing skills is part of the goal of using others' works. Instructors want you to learn to write and think, not just hand back what someone else created.

One way to develop paraphrasing skills is to read the material several times to make sure that you understand completely what the writer is saying. Next, put aside the author's work and try to explain the passage in your own words. This will help you develop a personal voice and style. Compare the explanation with the original and decide whether it is accurate and conveys the original ideas. Is something missing from your paraphrase that a person who hadn't read the source passage would need to know to understand it? If so, revise your paraphrase. It is vital that the paraphrase not alter the original meaning of the source. Adding words that distort the intention of the author or leave out significant parts can misstate or misrepresent what that author intended.

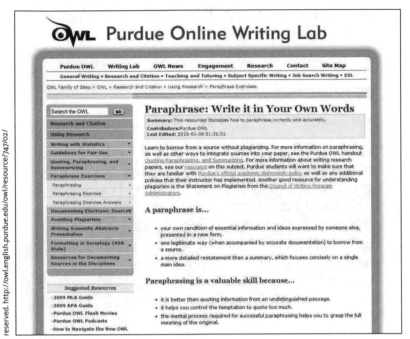

The OWL at Purdue University website has information to help you correctly paraphrase.

Also make sure to explain how the paraphrased content relates to your idea. Once you have worked the paraphrase into your draft, be sure to cite the original.

SAMPLE PARAPHRASES

Paraphrase with citation, MLA

Original work

Poll after poll indicates that one of the primary concerns of contemporary U.S. citizens is violence. Terrorism is obviously one part of this concern, but there is also considerable concern about non-terrorist forms of violence. Violence among the nation's youth is especially troubling and difficult to explain. This difficulty is frequently the reason that social psychologists are often asked to make sense of seemingly senseless acts of violence. Why are there so many shootings in the U.S. high schools? Why are there so many gangs, and why are they growing at such alarming rates? (Potter 306)

Incorrect paraphrase

Survey **after** survey show **that one of the** big things that people in the U.S. worry about today is **violence. Terrorism is** clearly a reason **but there is also** a lot of worry **about** other **forms of violence. Violence** from the young people in this country is very confusing **and** hard to understand. **This** problem is **often** the issue **that researchers** are frequently required to explain incomprehensible violent crimes. What is the reason for the number of gun related crimes in schools in America? Is it because the number **of gangs** are going up?

This paraphrase copies the content and writing style of the source passage. It is plagiarized, not paraphrased. Sentence by sentence, the information is exactly restated using different words. The substituted words in exact sequence are underlined. The sequence of each idea and structure of each sentence is the same, and words have been replaced with synonyms. In some cases, original phrases have been kept in order (shown in **bold**). This "patchwork paraphrasing" merely uses synonyms for words in the original text, but everything is essentially identical. Finally, there is no citation as the end of the paraphrase. Now consider the following:

Correct paraphrase

Many recent **polls** have suggested that people in the United States are very concerned about **terrorism** and other acts of violence. Increasing **violence,** including **shootings,** among **high-school-aged** children is one of these concerns. People in the community want to understand why this is happening. **Social psychologists** have been asked to explain this troubling trend. It is difficult to understand why young people may be joining **gangs** and committing acts of violence in greater numbers. (Potter 306)

This example—which uses MLA citation—maintains the ideas of the original piece, but the style of writing is different. Instead of following an identical sequence to the original work, the correctly paraphrased paragraph conveys the information but does not pull out words and substitute them with synonyms. It uses *some* of the words from the original to accurately present the author's ideas and is complete in presenting the original author's ideas, but it uses the student's original sentences. It also cites the author of the original work. The following is another example:

Paraphrase with citation, MLA

Original work

At first glance, there appears to be little justification for telling the story of California's early Indian wars. Aside from the brief Modoc conflict of 1873, and possibly the Mariposa war of 1851, few people are aware that California had any Indian troubles during the Gold Rush days of the 1850s. Certainly the Far West never had a Custer's Last Stand or a grand retreat such as that made by Chief Joseph of the Nez Perce. There were no Sitting Bull or Geronimo, no spectacular uprisings, like Adobe Walls or Beecher's Islands. On the contrary, many California tribes were generally peaceful by nature, few having even a war club or a tomahawk as part of their culture. Yet in California, the bloodiest drama in the settlement of the West took place, a brutal disruption and destruction so devastating that by the 1870s many native groups were extinct. (Secrest xi)

Incorrect paraphrase

<u>Unless you know about the events</u>, <u>you would think</u> <u>there isn't much reason to write about what happened</u> in the **Indian wars in early California.** There were two conflicts, one in 1873 with the **Modoc** and another in **Mariposa in 1851.** But most people don't know anything <u>about California having trouble with Indians during the</u> **1850s Gold Rush.** **The Far West** <u>didn't have any famous Indian conflicts like</u> **Custer's Last Stand** or any other Indians that were well known like **Chief Joseph of the Nez Perce, Sitting Bull, or Geronimo.** It <u>didn't have</u> Indian revolts like **Adobe Walls or Beecher's Islands.** <u>In California the Indians were peaceful and didn't carry weapons.</u> <u>But California had the</u> **bloodiest** <u>wars in the</u> **West**. <u>It was harsh and destructive and annihilated the Indians to the point where by the 1870s many of the groups were dead and gone</u>.

This paragraph is plagiarized. Notice that the writing style of the original piece was copied. Sentence by sentence the information is restated using different words, and the sequence of each idea is the same. In most cases, words have been substituted for synonyms (see <u>underlined</u>), while in others, words have been kept (see **bold**). This is another example of patchwork paraphrasing. In addition, no indication of the source of this paraphrase is provided in the text.

Correct paraphrase

If history books are to be believed, there is little to say about the California Indian conflicts. Indeed it would seem that all of the great battles such as Custer's Last Stand and the great chiefs were only far away. While history shows us the Gold Rush and its subsequent effect on California, it also leaves us with the false impression that California Indians were peaceful, with no weapons or conflicts with the intruding whites. This type of historical

omission negates the devastation and annihilation that
the California Indians suffered; annihilation so complete
"that by the 1870s many native groups were extinct"
(Secrest xi).

In this example, the ideas of the original piece are maintained,
but the style of writing is different and belongs to the writer
of the paper. Instead of following an identical sequence to the
original work, the correctly paraphrased paragraph conveys
the information. Once more, it does not use synonyms in
place of the original author's words. It still uses some of
the phrasing from the original, but this instance is identified
by quotation marks and is used to accurately convey and
emphasize the ideas of the original author. It also cites the
author of the original work using MLA style.

To avoid the errors of adding information that wasn't in the
original work or omitting something important to the original
meaning, carefully track your sources and acknowledge them
in your writing. You need to correctly present the meaning,
and you need to cite the source accurately. Sometimes it is
difficult to work with many different ideas, but remember
that your professor is very familiar with many of the ideas
and sources you'll use and can help you work out how best to
present them.

CITING PARAPHRASES

Like direct quotations, the only difference between APA and
MLA styles is the citation at the end.

MLA style includes the name of the author and the page
number. Use (N.pag) is if the page is unavailble

> . . . Yet in California, the bloodiest drama in the settlement
> of the West took place, a brutal disruption and destruction
> so devastating that by the 1870s many native groups were
> extinct (Secrest xi).

APA style includes the name of the author, the date of publication, and the page number.

> . . . Yet in California, the bloodiest drama in the settlement of the West took place, a brutal disruption and destruction so devastating that by the 1870s many native groups were extinct (Secrest, 2003, p. xi).

For electronic sources, consult the applicable style guide. What is important to know, however, is that you don't need to include page numbers because there aren't any. Your citation only needs the author's name (and the date if applicable) and points to the Works Cited or References list, where readers can find additional information—such as a URL—to check a source.

Tip

When citing online sources, you do not include the page numbers of your printout.

Knowledge Check

True or False?

1. Keeping the writing style of the original passage when you paraphrase is appropriate as long as you change most of the words. T/F

2. Correct paraphrasing includes a citation for the original source after the paraphrased passage. T/F

3. A paraphrase should be roughly the same length as the original. T/F

Check your answers on page 54.

5
Summarizing

DEFINING A SUMMARY

A **summary** condenses the size of an original piece of writing while retaining its author's essential message. A summary enables you to comment briefly on another writer's ideas and express how they relate to your own. Summarizing shortens the length of the original passage, whereas paraphrasing nearly matches the original in length.

To summarize another writer's passage, read it several times—taking notes if necessary—to make sure you understand what the writer is saying. It might help to read it aloud so you can hear the words. Then say to yourself, "In other words . . ." and complete the thought. If you use almost as many words to explain or express the thought, then you need to revise it and make it simpler and briefer. Reduce the original passage to its basic idea. And make sure to explain for your reader how the writer's idea relates to the point you are making in your paper.

> ## Tip
> *Do*
> 1. Be accurate to the original meaning.
> 2. Cite the original source.
> 3. Make your summary significantly shorter than the original.
> 4. Use your own words and explain how the writer's idea relates to yours.
>
> (*continued*)

Don't

1. Copy the original writing style; use your own.
2. Replace the original words with synonyms.
3. Change the meaning of a passage.

SAMPLE SUMMARY

Original work

Polls show that large majorities of Americans believe that anyone who works hard can succeed, and even higher percentages of Americans say they admire people who get rich by their own efforts. Those who fall behind, meanwhile, are often blamed for their misery. In a typical recent survey finding, three quarters of Americans agreed with the statement that if a person is poor, their own "lack of effort" is to blame. In other words, Americans tend to make moral judgments about people based upon their level of economic success. Everybody loves a winner, the saying goes, and nowhere is that more true than in America. Winners are seen as virtuous, as people to admire and emulate. Losers get the opposite treatment— for their own good, mind you. As Marvin Olasky, . . . has said: "An emphasis on freedom should also include a willingness to step away for a time and let those who have dug their own hole suffer the consequences of their misconduct." The prevalence of a sink-or-swim mentality in the United States is unique among Western democracies, as is the belief that individuals have so much control over their destiny. Elsewhere people are more apt to believe that success or failure is determined by circumstances beyond individual control. Scholars attribute the difference in outlook to the "exceptionalism" of America and, especially to the American Dream ethos

that dominates U.S. culture—an ethos at once intensely
optimistic and brutally unforgiving. (Callahan 124–25)

Incorrect summary

Polls show that large majorities of Americans believe that
anyone who works hard can succeed, and even higher
percentages of Americans say they admire people who get
rich by their own efforts. Winners are seen as virtuous, as
people to admire and emulate. Elsewhere people are more
apt to believe that success or failure is determined by
circumstances beyond individual control.

The above summary was created using the AutoSummarize
feature of Word set for 25%. It selects key sentences from the
original document and puts those sentences together to form
an abbreviated copy. (Note that the AutoSummarize feature is
intended for writers to provide summaries of their own work,
not the work of others.) This is not an acceptable summary
because it is entirely copied, word for word. It is plagiarism.
It does not change the writing style of the original author,
nor does it give credit with a correct citation to indicate the
source. Additional problems with this method of summary
may be the altering of the original meaning of the piece.
Note that the original piece was about the difference between
how Americans view winners and losers, but the summary
does not mention how losers are viewed. That thesis has not
been mentioned in the summary. It is important to connect a
summary to the point you are making in your paper and the
reason why you referred to the source you are summarizing.

Correct summary

According to Callahan, Americans, unlike people in other
Western democracies, take the moral perspective that
success is the result of individual effort. Most believe
that a person's success is a product of his or her labor and
thus deserved. Conversely, a person's poverty or failure is

viewed as the outcome of his or her lack of sufficient effort and is therefore also deserved (124–25).

In the correct summary, which uses MLA citation, the ideas of the original passage are maintained, but the style of writing is different from the original passage, and the summary is shorter than the original. In a paper, the summary should also clearly address your thesis or argument. It should convey the main points of the original, but it does not copy full sentences or substitute words with synonyms. It can have some material in common with the original as long as it accurately presents the author's ideas—and it should be cited correctly.

Knowledge Check

True or False?

1. You can keep the writing style of the original passage when you summarize as long as you significantly shorten the length and leave out some of the original. T/F

2. Correct summarizing includes a citation for the original source next to the summarized passage. T/F

3. A summary should convey the same meaning as the original. T/F

Check your answers on page 55.

6
References and Works Cited Lists

As you draft your paper, you will assemble a complete list of source materials that correlate with the quotations and paraphrases that you use. This list, as discussed in previous chapters, appears at the end of your paper. You will also need to format this list in the style required by your instructor.

This chapter presents the basics of formatting an **author-date** reference list in MLA and APA style. (Referencing sources with footnotes is not covered here. But if you want to learn more, consult the *Chicago Manual of Style*) The guidelines here will help get you started and make you aware of this important part of writing a paper. For additional information, you should consult the appropriate style guide. You can also get more help from your instructor, your school's library or writing center, and the online resources listed in Chapter 8.

CITATION CONTENT

While the information presented in all styles is the same, the order of the information and how it is shown can be quite different. The basic information contained by all citation styles includes the following:

• Author name

• Title of article, essay, book, or website

• Publisher information

• Year of publication

• Place or form of publication

BASIC FORMAT

All documentation styles place the list of references at the end of the paper. Follow these basic formatting rules for all citation styles:

- Arrange all citations in alphabetical order by the author's last name.

- Arrange authors' names in a multiple-author work exactly as they appear in the source.

- Reverse the author's name so that the last name appears first.

- Double-space your list of references, as you would your paper.

- Use a hanging indent so that the second and subsequent lines of a citation allow the author's name to appear by itself in the left margin. The typical indention is one-half inch (five spaces).

- Include in your list of references only the works to which your paper refers.

Tip

Always check with your instructor for the required documentation style.

MLA CITATIONS

Books

The basic elements of an MLA citation of a book include the following:

- Author name (last name, first name) followed by a period.

- *Book Title*—italicized, followed by a period.

- City of publication, followed by a colon.

- Publisher's name, followed by a comma. Use only the first name of the publisher, and abbreviate University Press to UP.

- Type of publication (Print, Web, Recording) followed by a period.

An example of a single-author book is presented below:

Downing, Skip. *On Course*. Boston: Houghton Mifflin, 2008. Print.

Multiple authors

When you are citing a book that has two or three authors, list them in the order in which they appear on the title page. Invert the first author's name (last name first), but not the names of the second or third author. Separate all the authors by commas. For a book by four or more authors, MLA allows the listing to include either all the authors listed in order or just the first author followed by the Latin words **et al.**, which is short for *et alia*, meaning "and others." Check with your instructor about the form that he or she prefers.

The following example is for a book by two authors:

Schein, Elyse, and Paula Bernstein. *Identical Strangers*. New York: Random House, 2007. Print.

These examples are for a book with four or more authors:

Kauffman, James, Mark Mostert, Stanley Trent, and Daniel Hallahan. *Managing Classroom Behavior*. Boston: Allyn & Bacon, 2002. Print.

or

Kauffman, James, et al. *Managing Classroom Behavior*. Boston: Allyn & Bacon, 2002. Print.

Articles or essays

You might use an article from a periodical or an essay from an anthology. While the basic structure of citations for articles is the same as for books, there are some significant differences. You need to list both the title of the article or essay, the journal or book in which it was published, and the page range.

The information in a citation of a source from an anthology follows this order:

- Author of the article or essay (last name first) followed by a period.

- "Title of the article or essay" in quotation marks, followed by a period.

- *Title of the Book*—italicized, followed by a period.

- Comp. (for "compiled by") or Ed. (for "edited by").

- Author of the book (first name first), followed by a period.

- City, followed by a colon.

- Publisher, followed by a comma.

- Year, followed by a period.

- Page range (separated by a hyphen or en dash) followed by a period.

- The word "Print," followed by a period (if your instructor is using the *MLA Handbook for Writers of Research Papers,* 7th ed.).

Anson, Chris. "Taking Off." *Finding Our Way: A Writing Teacher's Sourcebook.* Ed. Wendy Bishop and Deborah Coxwell Teague. Boston: Houghton Mifflin, 2005. 44–51. Print.

Tip

Citations from an anthology or magazine should include the page numbers.

Popular magazine and newspaper articles include the month, either spelled out or abbreviated, of publication in the citation.

Smith, Julian. "Endangered Destinations." *U.S. News and World Report.* May 2008: 36–43. Print.

For scholarly journals, the volume number is included after the journal title. The year is placed in parentheses. A colon follows the year and the page range.

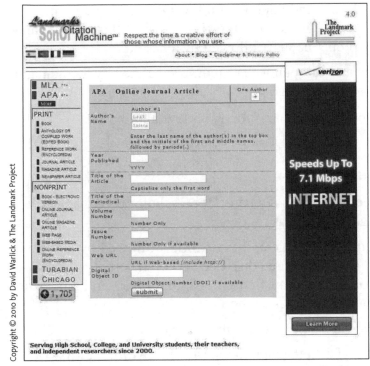

Landmark's Citation Machine makes preparing references in different styles easy.

Houston, Linda "Teaching English in the Two Year College." *Urbana* 35 (2008): 323–26. Print.

APA CITATIONS

The APA style contains the same information as MLA, but it formats the content differently, putting more emphasis on the date of publication.

Books

The basic APA style of citation for a book is as follows:

* Author (last name first) then first initial, followed by a period. For a work by more than one author, invert all names, use initials instead of first names, and insert an ampersand (&) before the last author.

* Year of publication in parentheses, followed by a period.

- Book title and volume number *italicized* (capitalize the first word of the title, the first word of the subtitle, and any proper nouns), followed by a period.

- City and full publisher's name, separated by a colon and followed by a period.

The following example is for a single-author book:

Buckland, R. (2002). *The Witch Book*. Detroit: Visible Ink.

Articles

The basic APA style of citation for a scholarly journal article by a single author is as follows:

- Author last name and first initial followed by a period. For a work by more than one author, invert all names, use initials instead of first names, and insert an ampersand (&) before the last author.

- Year (in parentheses) with a period.

- Title of article (capitalize only first word, the first word after a colon, and any proper nouns; and no quotation marks), followed by a period.

- Title of journal in *italics,* followed by a comma.

- Volume number in *italics,* followed by a comma.

- Issue number in *parentheses* (3). Followed by a comma.

- Full page range of article, followed by a period.

Here is an example of a journal article by a single author:

Houston, L. (2008). Teaching english in the two year college. *Urbana, 35,* 323–26.

For a journal article by two to five authors, use the following example as a guideline:

Brown, C., A., Dickson, R., Humphreys, A., McQuillan, V. & Smears, E. (2008). Promoting academic writing/referencing skills: Outcome of an undergraduate e-learning pilot project. *British Journal of Educational Technology, 39,* 140.

MLA AND APA CITATIONS FOR WEB PUBLICATIONS

In earlier editions of the *MLA Handbook*, including the URLs of websites and sources was recommended in Works Cited entries. Because websites often change and web addresses can be cumbersome, including URLs is now optional. As always, check what your instructor requires for proper formatting. If you do include a URL, it is placed after the date of access, a period then a space. Always use angle brackets to enclose the URL with a period at the end of the entry (*MLA* Handbook 182).

Provide the following information for Web publications and similar electronic sources. This example uses those elements listed by the MLA. APA style includes most of these with some exceptions.

- Author, director, editor, performer, etc. of work (if available)
- Title of full work (if available), set in quotations marks if the work is part of a larger work, and italicized if the work is independent
- Title of overall website set in italics
- Date of work (if available)
- Name of institution/organization that sponsors the site
- Date of publication (day, month, and year) n.d. if no date available
- Web (type of publication)
- Date of access
- Optional: URL (set in angle brackets (< >))

MLA online citation

The MLA citation shows the author's full name and the date after the title. Note that the year of publication is followed by a period, that the date of access is day, month (abbreviated, except May) and that no punctuation follows it. The word "Web" precedes the access date and is separated by a period.

The final element is the URL, which is set in angle brackets. For longer Web addresses, the line break of the URL falls after a slash, and a period closes the entry.

The following example is for an MLA Web publication citation with an author:

Warlick, David. "Landmarks Son of A Citation Machine." *The Landmark Project*. 2009. Web. 19 Mar. 2005 <http://www.citationmachine.net>.

For an online citation without an author, the title replaces the author as the element that is alphabetized in the Works Cited list, as shown in the following example, which has other differences. Here the sponsor of the website is listed. Note again the placement of the medium (Web), access date, and URL.

DSPS Student Programs and Services, 2003. Santa Barbara City College. Web. 3 Jan. 2004 <http://www.sbcc.edu/dsps/>.

APA online citation

APA electronic citations follow the rules of normal APA style of formatting such as capitalization, first initial, year placement, and italics. Note that the retrieval date is spelled out, that a comma follows it, and that no punctuation follows the URL. The full URL is normally given. This example shows an article that has an author:

Lee. I. (1998). *A Research Guide for Students: Research, Writing, and Style Guides*. Retrieved March 19, 2005, from http://www.aresearchguide. com/styleguides.html

This next example shows an online citation without an author:

DSPS policies and procedures. (2003). Santa Barbara City College. Retrieved January 3, 2004, from http://www.sbcc.edu/dsps/

Tip

Both APA and MLA Web publication citations require the date of access because websites often change, are archived, or even disappear from the Web.

TYPES OF REFERENCE LISTS

This section features examples of an MLA Works Cited
list, including the Works Cited list for publications used as
examples in this book. Consult your instructor as to whether
to use underline or italics.

MLA Works Cited list

Works Cited

Anson, Chris. "Taking Off." *Finding Our Way: A Writing Teacher's
    Sourcebook.* Ed. Wendy Bishop and Deborah Coxwell Teague.
    Boston: Houghton Mifflin, 2005. 44–51. Print.
Buckland, R. (2002). *The Witch Book.* Detroit: Visible Ink. Print.
DSPS Policies and Procedures, 2003. Santa Barbara City College. Web. 3
    Jan. 2004 <http://www.sbcc.edu/dsps/>.
Kauffman, James, Mark Mostert, Stanley Trent, and Daniel Hallahan.
    Managing Classroom Behavior. Boston: Allyn & Bacon, 2002.
    Print.
Schein, Elyse, and Paula Bernstein. *Identical Strangers.* New York:
    Random House, 2007. Print.
Smith, Julian. "Endangered Destinations." *U.S. News and World Report*
    May 2008: 36–43. Print.
Warlick, David. "Landmarks Citation Machine." *The Landmark Project.*
    2000. Web. 19 Mar. 2005 <http://citationmachine.net/>.

APA References list

References

Brown, C., A., Dickson, R., Humphreys, A., McQuillan, V. & Smears, E.
    (2008). Promoting Academic Writing/Referencing Skills: Outcome
    of an Undergraduate E-Learning Pilot Project. *British Journal of
    Educational Technology.* 39, 140.
DSPS Policies and Procedures. (2003). Santa Barbara City College.
    Retrieved January 3, 2004, from http://www.sbcc.edu/dsps/
Houston, L. (2008). Teaching English in the Two Year College. *Urbana,*
    35, 323–26.
Lee, I. (1998). *A Research Guide for Students: Research, Writing, and Style
    Guides.* Retrieved March 19, 2005, from http://www.aresearchguide
    .com/styleguides.html

Knowledge Check

True or False?

1. Works Cited or References lists should be single-spaced. T/F

2. Only works actually cited in the body of the paper should be listed in the Works Cited page. T/F

3. Works Cited or Reference lists should be listed in alphabetical order by author's last name. T/F

Check your answers on page 55.

7
Practice Quiz

1. **Cheating may include**

   a. plagiarizing or copying without attribution.

   b. using an essay or paper from someone who has previously taken the course.

   c. using answers to an exam from someone who has previously taken the course.

   d. all of the above.

2. **Plagiarism is**

   a. quoting someone else's work and giving credit to them.

   b. using someone else's ideas, work, sentences, research, or information and presenting it as your own.

   c. using original ideas in your written work.

   d. using Web sources.

3. **Citation of sources is required**

   a. whenever paraphrasing or summarizing an idea.

   b. only in the Works Cited section of your paper.

   c. when using your own ideas in an original paragraph.

   d. a and b

4. **The word *paraphrase* means**

   a. to replace original words with synonyms.

   b. to maintain the writing style of the original author.

   c.   to give an exact idea of the original author's meaning in your own writing style.

   d.   to give a general, but not exact, idea of the original author's meaning.

5. **A paragraph is not properly paraphrased when**

   a.   only a few words are different.

   b.   you express in your own words the general idea of what the author is saying.

   c.   the sentences have been rearranged but not changed much.

   d.   a and b

   e.   a and c

6. **Correct summarizing includes**

   a.   a copy of the original writing style.

   b.   replacing the original work with synonyms.

   c.   the accurate meaning of the original work but significantly shorter than the original.

   d.   using the auto-summarize feature of your word processing program.

7. **Citation of sources is required**

   a.   when quoting a source in your paper that you use word for word.

   b.   when browsing the Internet.

   c.   when describing another writer's idea in your paper.

   d.   a and c

8. **Over-quoting in your work**

   a.   shows you have not synthesized or analyzed the material from your resources.

   b.   is acceptable because it shows the amount of work and research you have done.

c.   means using too many direct quotes from your sources.

d.   a and c

e.   a and b

9. **John's paper is based on several different sources, including a research paper from a friend who took the same class last summer. Seeing that his friend's research closely matches his own, does John need to cite his friend in his final draft?**

a.   No, he just needs to cite the other sources.

b.   Yes, anything John consulted needs to be cited.

10. **Look at the original and choose which paraphrase is correct.**

Original

Because there are many ways to cheat, and there is temptation to do so, students may assume that this is something that everyone is doing. Surveys of college students show that cheating is a common occurrence, and some students consider it an accomplishment to get away with this type of behavior. These kinds of attitudes and behaviors are unethical and have consequences. (Menager, 2003, 12)

a.   Students can be tempted to cheat by the many resources available to them that make it easy. They may believe that a majority of students cheat in some form or another. Surveys done in colleges suggest that cheating is more rampant than once thought and that students see it as a triumph to cheat and not get caught. This shows a serious lack of ethics in behavior and can lead to repercussions from the academic institution (Menager, 2003, 12).

b.   Because there are so many different ways to cheat, and temptations for students are great, a lot of students think everyone is doing it. Students surveyed say that cheating is a common occurrence and it is an accomplishment to get away with it. This kind of attitude is unethical and can have some consequences.

8
Additional Sources of Information

Reference the following Web and print resources to learn more about plagiarism and proper citation using the various styles in use at institutions of higher learning in the United States, Canada, and elsewhere.

CITATION STYLE OVERVIEWS

University of California–Berkeley: Citing Your Sources

http://www.lib.berkeley.edu/instruct/guides/citations.html

DOCUMENTATION STYLES BY DISCIPLINE

Anthropology

http://www.aaanet.org/publications/guidelines.cfm

Law

http://www.law.cornell.edu/citation/?

Physics

http://www.aip.org/pubservs/style.html

Sociology

http://owl.english.purdue.edu/owl/resource/583/01/

FREE CITATION GENERATORS

Son of Citation Machine

http://www.citationmachine.net

Style Wizard

http://www.stylewizard.com

REFERENCE TRACKING

EasyBib

http://easybib.com

RefWorks

http://www.refworks.com

PLAGIARISM

University of Indiana: Plagiarism

http://www.indiana.edu/~istd/definition.html

Center for Academic Integrity

http://www.academicintegrity.org

Turnitin®.com

http://www.turnitin.com

Samford University Library

http://samford.libguides.com/content.php?pid=49052&sid=0

Scan My Essay

http://www.scanmyessay.com

Turn it in Safely

http://www.Turnitinsafely.com

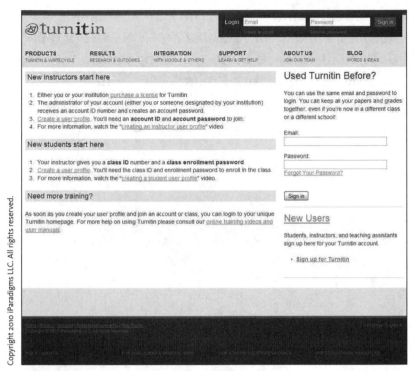

This is the page for establishing a Turnitin account and posting papers to check for authenticity.

STYLE GUIDES

American Psychological Association. *Publication manual of the American Psychological Association*. 6. Washington DC: APA, 2009. Print.

http://www.apastyle.org

The Chicago Manual of Style. 15. Chicago IL: University of Chicago Press, 2003. Print.

http://www.chicagomanualofstyle.org/home.html

The MLA Handbook for Writers of Research Papers. 7. New York: MLA, 2009. Print.

http://www.mla.org/store/CID24/PID363

Scientific Style and Format: The CSE Manual for Authors, Editors, and Publishers. 7. New York NY: Council of Science Editors in cooperation with The Rockefeller University Press, 2006. Print.

http://www.councilscienceeditors.org

Works Cited

Byrne, Robert. *The 2,548 Best Things Anybody Ever Said*. New York: Galahad, 1996. sec. 453. Print.

Callahan, David. *The Cheating Culture*. Florida: Harcourt, 2004. Print.

Chavez, J. Carolina. "Copyright's 'Elephant in the Room': A Realistic Look at the Role of Moral Rights in Modern American Copyright." Washington, D.C.: *American Intellectual Property Law Association Quarterly Journal*, 36 (2008): 125–45. Print.

Covey, Stephen. *The Seven Habits of Highly Effective People*. New York: Simon, 1989.97, 186. Print.

Houston, Linda "Teaching English in the Two Year College." *Urbana* 35 (2008): 323–26. Print.

Kauffman, James, Mark Mostert, Stanley Trent, and Daniel Hallahan. *Managing Classroom Behavior*. Boston: Allyn, 2002. Print.

Lathrop, Ann, and Kathleen Foss. *Student Cheating and Plagiarism in the Internet Era: A Wake-up Call*. Englewood, Colorado: Libraries Unlimited, 2000. Print.

Lipson, Charles, Doing *Honest Work in College: How to prepare citations, avoid plagiarism, and achieve real academic success*. Chicago, 2004. 36. Print.

Melville, Herman. Quotation 4797 in *Cole's Quotables*. Web. 30 Mar. 2005 <http://www.quotationspage.com/quote/4797.html>.

Potter, W. James. "Is Media Violence Harmful to Children?" *On Media Violence*. Thousand Oaks: Sage, 1999. [Rept in Brent Slife, *Taking Sides: Clashing on Controversial Psychological Issues*, 13th ed.] New York: McGraw, 2004. 306. Print.

Readers Digest Great Encyclopedic Dictionary: Standard College Dictionary 2nd Ed. New York: Funk & Wagnalls, 1967. 1031. Print.

Secrest, William B. *When the Great Spirit Died: Destruction of the California Indians, 1850–1860*. Sanger, California: Word Dancer, 2003. Print.

Schein, Elyse, and Paula Bernstein. *Identical Strangers*. New York: Random House, 2007. Print.

Weeks, Dudley. *The Eight Essential Steps to Conflict Resolution*. New York: Penguin, 1994.33. Print.

Zaharoff, Howard. "A Writer's Guide to Fair Use in Copyright Law." *Writers Digest* Jan. 2001. Web. 3 Mar. 2005 <http://www.writersdigest.com/ articles/zaharoff fair_copyright_law.asp>.

Answers to Exercises

Chapter 1

1. (True) Don't be one of them. This can be a costly mistake!

2. (False) It is your job to find out.

3. (False) All sources should be cited.

Chapter 2

1. (True) Most people who plagiarize use poor time management and even worse judgment.

2. (False) If you quote more than 10 percent of your paper, you may be graded down for overquoting.

3. (False) Using a friend's paper or an Internet paper is plagiarizing and considered to be academic cheating.

Chapter 3

1. (True) Quotations should be identical to the original passage.

2. (False) Block quotations do not require quotation marks.

3. (True) Brackets show that text was added to the original passage.

Chapter 4

1. (False) This is a common mistake students make because they don't know the rules and they lack confidence in their own writing ability. You should restate the writer's idea in your own words.

2. (True) Always acknowledge when you've used ideas from someone else, no matter whether it's a clause, sentence, or paragraph.

3. (True) A paraphrase restates another person's idea in your own words.

Chapter 5

1. (False) A summary should be in your own words and writing style but convey the message of the original. Do not use auto-summarize for someone else's work because it is just an abridged copy.

2. (True) Always acknowledge when you've used ideas from someone else, no matter what.

3. (True) Do not alter the meaning; just express it concisely and in your own words.

Chapter 6

1. (False) All references should be double-spaced.

2. (True)

3. (True)

Chapter 7

1. d   2. b   3. a   4. c   5. e   6. c   7. d   8. d   9. b
10. a